THE FATHER OF CHICAGO

DU SABLE

by Lois C. Beh

To Sally & Jim —
Such good friends!
Lois

THE FATHER OF CHICAGO

DU SABLE

Copyright © 2015 by Lois C. Beh

Passport Press
PassportPressBooks@gmail.com

Book design by Greg Morrill

Printed in the United States of America

ISBN: 978-0-9641328-1-8

PREFACE

Jean Baptiste Pointe du Sable, 1745-1818, a black man, native of Santo Domingo, arrived in the New World as it was being formed. He lived through turbulent and historic times. He developed property at the gateway between the Great Lakes and the Gulf of Mexico. That gateway is called Chicago – a major city of the world. His name has become more prominent in recent years and he is now credited as being the Father of Chicago. In 2010, the Michigan Avenue Bridge was renamed the Du Sable Bridge and a bronze bust of him installed on the northeast side of the bridge in Pioneer Plaza where his home once stood.

This story follows du Sable's adventures from a near drowning in a shipwreck, to living in New Orleans, poling up the Mississippi River to St. Louis, learning the trading post business, living with the Potawatomi Indians in St. Joseph, Michigan, and marrying a Potawatomi woman. He built a trading post near the bank of the Chicago River and Lake Michigan. During the Revolutionary War, he was captured and spent three years in Fort Mackinac as a prisoner of the British.

After the war ended, in 1783, du Sable returned to Chicago to expand his trapping and trading business. In 1800, he sold his property and moved to Peoria, Illinois and later to St. Charles, Missouri where he died and was buried in 1818.

Because little is known about du Sable's early life, this story blends fact and fiction to imagine what it might have been like to travel alongside du Sable through his adventures.

As you will see, he lived a life full of courage, excitement and accomplishment.

DEDICATION

To those who love Chicago.

TABLE OF CONTENTS

PREFACE

CHAPTER 1

LOST AND FOUND

Was this his day to die? Gulping his breath, he prayed, "Lord, don't let me die.

Lord, don't let me die!" Over and over and over, he repeated this prayer, "Lord, PLEASE don't let me die!"

The roaring waves continuously slammed into the makeshift raft as seawater splashed over him, chilling him to the bone.

Hours passed before the waters calmed and the waves began to roll more gently under his crate. At last the black storm clouds parted and a wondrously clear sky appeared. An endless sweep of brilliant stars sparkled above him. There was no sound now but the lapping of water. Jean drifted on, not knowing where the sea was taking him. The crate moved in a slow rocking motion. Finally, he lost consciousness.

When Jean Baptiste Pointe du Sable opened his eyes, he was in a bed with white sheets. A tall, slender woman in a long, blue dress was standing at his side holding his hand.

"Are you feeling better?" She asked the question in French, which was her native language, as well as what Jean spoke and understood. "I am Sister Mary Francois."

The nurse had a beautiful face, dark eyebrows arching over large brown eyes that were full of kindness. Her voice was gentle as she said, "You are in the French Royal Hospital in the village of New Orleans. Your ship capsized and sank to the bottom of

1

the sea. Fisherman rescued you and brought you to the hospital. We are unaware of other survivors."

No other survivors? Jean could hardly comprehend the news. No captain, no shipmates? I'm the only one alive from our crew? This was unbelievable! Tears burned in Jean's eyes and ran down his cheeks as he began to sob uncontrollably. His head throbbed. His body ached. He was so far away from home. What would he do now? He didn't know anyone and felt so completely alone. Why was I the only one to survive? He asked himself, again and again.

"I am so very sorry," whispered Sister Mary Francois. "We will take care of you until you feel better." She gently squeezed his hand.

CHAPTER 2

DU SABLE'S EARLY DAYS

Jean Baptiste Pointe du Sable was born about 1745 in Santo Domingo, a small island between the Atlantic Ocean and the Caribbean Sea.

He was raised an only child by his black, free-slave mother and his French, seafaring father. They lived in a one-room, thatched-roof cottage by the sea. The climate was warm, the language French, and the religions Catholic and voodoo.

By the time Jean was five years old, he would slip out of the house first thing in the morning and run to watch the fisherman drag their boats through the wet sand to the water. At sunset he looked forward to seeing the catch of the day. What he found most

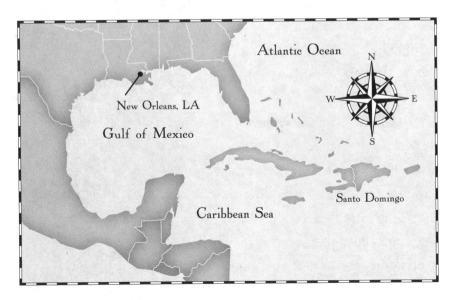

exciting were the days when the big ships with billowing sails from far-off seas came to rest in their small harbor. He parked himself cross-legged on the bank near the dock and listened to the voices of the men calling to one another in languages unknown to him. He helped the sailors unload their ships, ran errands for them, and took them to find food and drink. With his ready smile and warm personality, he was well liked by the men. They often gave him coins or tokens from their travels.

As he grew older and his fascination with the big ships increased, he spent more time with the sailors. He often helped with needed repairs, earning himself a first-hand look at what it would be like to live on a ship.

His well-traveled sailor friends talked of the New World, a country across the sea north of Santo Domingo. They told of people from Europe who were moving there; people from Spain, England, and France searching for land and freedom in areas claimed by their countries. Hearing stories of these adventurers, Jean resolved that someday he, too, would travel aboard a ship to the New World.

His father was a seaman who left home as a young man. He shared his son's desire to explore new horizons. When Jean turned 17, his father said to him, "You are older than I was when I left home, my son. If you think you are ready to travel the world, go with my blessing. Seek the adventure you are looking for, but come back to us if you don't find it."

That same year, in 1762, with his worldly possessions carefully packed in a wooden box, Jean boarded a ship that would take him to the New World. The captain agreed to include him as part of the crew.

The morning of his departure, his mother, with tears in her eyes said, "Jean, I want you to have this medal of my favorite saint. I pray that it will help to keep you safe."

Jean accepted the medal with its chain and hung it around his neck.

"I love you, Mother, and I will wear it always." Jean gave his mother a kiss.

He said farewell to parents and friends and watched his mother hide her sadness to soften the sting of his leaving. In the distance, he heard the choir of young voices singing hymns beneath the roof of his village church. He felt the lump in his throat as he waved. It seemed he had always dreamed of this day. Yet, now that it was here, he was unsure. With a mixture of sadness at leaving home and the expectation of what lay ahead, he entered the life of a sailor. Was he doing the right thing? Was there time for him to change his mind? Jean was asking himself these questions when the captain shouted the order for the men to pull up the anchor and cast off the shore lines. The ship started its move out of the port. Jean watched the faces of loved ones, the small fishing boats, and the mountains until they all melted away.

They sailed in good weather until the morning the ship neared the Port of New Orleans, Louisiana. Just off the coast, threatening clouds gathered, blocking their view of land. A brutal storm broke loose. Lightning zigzagged across the darkening sky. Huge gusts of wind battered the ship off course. White-capped waves broke over the bow lifting and slamming the ship down. The cracks of thunder were deafening. Crates broke from their moorings and slid across the surface of the deck. The captain could not see the surface of the sea in front of him. The ship was taking on water. "Grab any container." the captain yelled. "Start bailing! Work fast or we drown!"

This was a scene of terror and confusion, some men screaming in fear, others praying out loud. The terrified men worked to the point of exhaustion as the ship continued to roll violently. Then one towering wave pitched the vessel on its side hurling all on board into the dark sea. Jean, struggling, swam to a large wooden crate that was floating nearby, and with a hidden reserve of energy, pulled himself on top of it. He quickly secured himself with some rope attached to the sides of the crate and clung to the tossing makeshift raft.

CHAPTER 3

NEW ORLEANS, LOUISIANA

After being rescued by the fisherman, Jean regained his strength, thanks to the support and kindly attention he received. Knowing that he had no place to go, the sisters invited him to stay and help with the building of a new addition to the hospital. In return, they gave him a room and meals and an opportunity to learn from one of the area's best woodcrafters.

In his free time, he crisscrossed the rutted streets of New Orleans, mingling with the immigrants, mules and wagons that crowded the town. As the darkening skies of evening approached, a different, noisy sort of people roamed the area; trappers, sailors and traders, looking to cheer their spirits. Waterfront cafes and smoke-filled bars rang with the musical mixture of trumpets, strings, and pianos luring the passersby inside.

Jean lingered in a dark alleyway by a particular bar, enjoying the rhythmic notes that an old Negro fiddler, by the name of Black Dog Jules, played each evening. One night the fiddler came to the door. Jean was afraid he was going to send him away, but instead he smiled and said, "Come in here, young man, and sit on this stool near the stage. I've seen you hanging around here night after night. I like it when somebody takes to my performance style.

Would you like to learn to play this thing?" Jules pointed to the fiddle.

Shocked at the invitation, Jean said, "I would love to try."

So on Wednesday evenings when Jean's job at the hospital was finished and before Black Dog Jules' work began, Jean received a fiddle lesson. He never became what one would call accomplished, but he learned to play well enough to entertain himself and friends.

One day in the town square Jean saw a note tacked to a tree inviting townpeople to a public hanging of an escaped slave. Next to that sign this notification was posted:

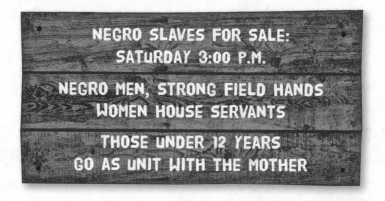

NEGRO SLAVES FOR SALE:
SATURDAY 3:00 P.M.

NEGRO MEN, STRONG FIELD HANDS
WOMEN HOUSE SERVANTS

THOSE UNDER 12 YEARS
GO AS UNIT WITH THE MOTHER

Jean could hardly believe what he was reading! He had never seen a hanging or the selling and buying of African slaves. In fact he, Jean Baptiste Pointe du Sable, had the dark skin color of these slaves because he looked more like his mother's family than the French ancestors of his father.

Blood rose to his face, and his heart began to pound in his chest as he reached up and tried to pull the sign down. Almost immediately Jean felt a large, hard hand on his shoulder. "What do you think you are doin', BLACK BOY?" a loud, deep-throated voice bellowed in his ear. Jean turned around to see a big, burly, white man with small angry eyes and a deep scar that ran down the side of his bloated face pushing against him.

"I am taking this ugly sign down," Jean said.

"Well, I suggest you leave that sign alone, BLACK BOY, unless you want to be the first one on the block to be sold." The man gave Jean a hearty shove. In reaction, Jean flung his arm around and hit the man on the side of his face. The man grabbed and twisted Jean's arm to the point of breaking it, and shouted, "You show your face again, and mark my words, you won't walk from here." In silent fury Jean stalked away, vowing to leave New Orleans as soon as possible.

He headed for the bank of the Mississippi River. The area was always bustling and congested with boats of all sizes that had arrived from the north, loaded with grain and bundles of animal skins. On return trips the boats were filled with barrels of food, guns, traps, and other supplies needed by those living up north. During the time Jean had been in New Orleans, he made friends with some men who traveled the river by canoe from St. Louis.

Maybe I could join one of these crews and get away from here, Jean thought.

By the large bonfire down at the river's edge, groups of people gathered to listen to the boatmates talk freely of their wild and often frightening adventures with animals and Native Indians. On that evening Jean met Jacques Little Fox, a boatman with wide shoulders, powerful arms and legs as big as tree stumps. Bushy eyebrows hovered over squinty brown eyes. His cheekbones were high and his face darkly tanned. He had a booming voice and a laugh that bounced off the hills. Jacques had a love and respect for the river, the woods, and life itself. Jean knew that Jacques had the reputation as being the best pilot on the Mississippi River.

Jean heard stories of how fortunes were made by trapping and trading. Wealthy people on the East Coast and in Europe were willing to pay a lot of money for luxurious fur hats and coats. The best pelts were coming from the unsettled lands north of New Orleans.

ANIMAL PELTS

Beaver, badger, bear, buffalo, deer, elk, fox, mink, muskrat, otter, porcupine, possum, rabbit, skunk, squirrel, weasel, and wolf were among the animals trapped for their fur.

"Jean," said Jacques, "I have been aware of you listening to our stories and you seem interested. I could use a hand like you. Why not join us on our next trip up to St. Louis? We leave the day after tomorrow at four in the morning. Think it over. We will have a good time."

Still angry, Jean didn't need to think it over. "I will be there, Jacques."

The morning they were leaving New Orleans, Jacques Little Fox issued instructions to the men who had signed up to join him.

"I have a few basic rules that we live by," he said. "We do not complain, and we never keep anyone waiting. As for me, I promise you a fresh new scene at every bend of the river."

Jean could hardly contain his excitement, yet he knew that his strength and maturity would soon be tested.

Dawn crept across the water as the last bundle was tucked into the boat called a pirogue. Jean took with him the fiddle from Black Dog Jules and a slender bag of necessities. Jacques Little Fox handed each man a wooden paddle and a 12-foot pole that they used to push away from the shore by jabbing the poles into the riverbed and bending and pushing their bodies to propel the boat forward.

In no time, huge blisters appeared on Jean's hands. His back, his legs, his neck, everything hurt as ever so slowly they moved up the river. In the days that followed, his hands and body began to toughen to the task. The more experienced of his boatmates found ways of passing time by telling long, detailed stories, old jokes, and singing favorite travel songs, over and over. This was one of his favorites:

"We begun, a day or two ago,

It seems a month and it's goin' slow

But friends we are a singin' as we dip and paddle full

We'll be glad to get our feet on ground so PULL, PULL, PULL."

Weather permitting they pushed off from each campsite before dawn traveling three or four hours before the first of their two meals. They continued with measured strokes of the paddles into the evening. Before nightfall when they set foot on land, the men gathered wood and built a campfire. Dinner usually consisted of biscuits, fish, berries, and other edibles they found along the way.

PIROGUE

A boat called a dugout canoe or as the French called it a pirogue, was crafted by cutting down, burning out, hollowing, and shaping the trunk of a tree, some more than 50 feet long.

They laughed and told funny stories of the day's adventures. Jean played his fiddle until the embers of the fire died down. Then they wrapped themselves in buffalo skin blankets and bedded on pine boughs for much needed sleep. On stormy nights the men huddled together in small bark and stick shelters they fashioned or under the unloaded pirogue.

There were times when the Mississippi River was rebellious. The men struggled against the swift current and contended with submerged rocks, downed trees, beaver dams, high winds, blistering sun, rain, and lots of mosquitoes. Often they had to get out of the boat onto the shore and with long ropes and strong backs pull the boat around rocks and debris. Jean was glad to be away from New Orleans and in the company of seasoned travelers.

CHAPTER 4

ST. LOUIS, MISSOURI

After months of sweat and strain, the long, tedious journey came to an end. The men finally reached their destination of St. Louis, Missouri. Before nightfall they unloaded the boat and carried their cargo up the hill to the trading post. Jacques Little Fox was paid and handed out the share of wages to the men. The boatmates headed for the saloon, but Jean Baptiste Pointe du Sable was more interested in knowing where he was going to sleep. Jacques Little Fox took Jean to a rooming house and introduced him to Etta Jones, the owner. Etta was less than five feet tall but sturdy, with white hair pulled back in a bun at the nape of her neck. She eyed Jean with suspicion.

"So, you're a friend of Jacques. Jacques is a good boy and I 'spect you to be too. No cussin', drinkin', and stayin' out late. Take your things to the bedroom in the back of the house." Jean did as he was told, then joined his friends at the saloon for the much anticipated home-cooked meal.

Jacques put his arm around Jean's shoulder. "I like you, du Sable. You're a good hand to have on board. How about coming back to New Orleans with me? I know it took us three months to get here, but the trip down river will only take us ten days to two weeks. The wind and the current pushes us right down to New Orleans."

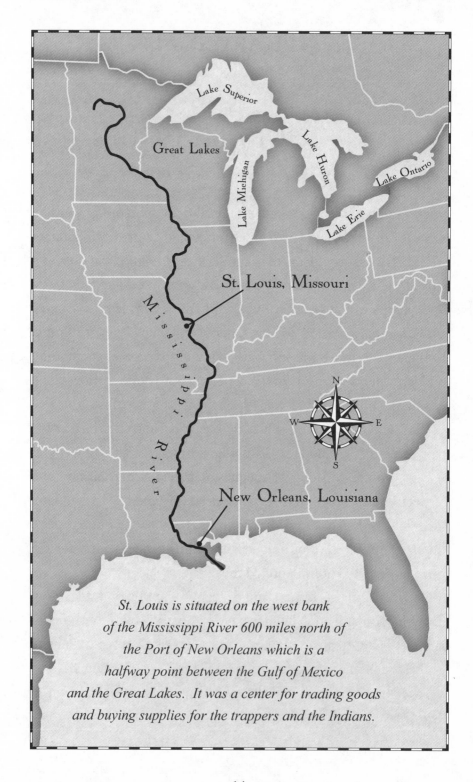

Lake Superior

Great Lakes

Lake Michigan

Lake Huron

Lake Ontario

Lake Erie

St. Louis, Missouri

Mississippi River

N

W   E

S

New Orleans, Louisiana

*St. Louis is situated on the west bank
of the Mississippi River 600 miles north of
the Port of New Orleans which is a
halfway point between the Gulf of Mexico
and the Great Lakes. It was a center for trading goods
and buying supplies for the trappers and the Indians.*

"I appreciate the offer, but poling up the Mississippi from New Orleans once is enough for me," Jean said. "Thank you, Jacques, but no. I think I will stay here for awhile."

Jean was now 20 years old, living in St. Louis and looking for work. As luck would have it, by the middle of the following week, Henri Fontour, the owner of a St. Louis trading post gave Jean a job. Henry was tall and wiry. His eyes were so deep set that it was hard to guess how he viewed the world about him. This, coupled with a droopy red mustache that hung two inches below his chin, gave the impression that he didn't want anyone to know what he was thinking. Yet he had a reputation as an honorable tradesman, which Jean soon found was rare among those who dealt with the Native Indians.

TRADE GOODS

Axes, blankets, bullets, colorful glass beads, fish hooks, kettles, knives, muskets, needles, traps, and woven cloth were among trade goods desired.

For hundreds of years, the Indians' only weapons and hunting tools had been bows and arrows and spears. Now they wanted what the white man used: firearms, gunpowder, and steel knives. They found what they needed at the trading post.

The beaver pelt was standard currency. Articles for trade were evaluated by the number of skins they would bring. For example:

1 beaver = 1 blanket
1 beaver = 1 brass kettle
1 beaver = 2 boxes of tobacco
1 beaver = 1 steel knife
2 beaver = 1 pound of colorful glass beads
12 beaver = 14-foot musket (rifle)

When spring arrived, St Louis bulged with a mixture of rough adventurers and traders. This wild mix of humanity gathered after the long, cold, isolating winter to trade and blow off steam. When they arrived in St. Louis from the wilderness, they had not bathed for months. Their clothes were covered with grease from the meat they ate. If they wanted shorter hair, they singed it off or pulled it out, hair by hair. Some were educated, others couldn't write their names; some were religious, others, outlaws. But they all knew how to raise a riot after a winter of isolation and deprivation. At any time of the day or night, one could hear whooping, fighting, and cursing. Sometimes gunfire rocked the air. More than once Jean witnessed some shaggy, bearded soul fly out of the swinging doors of the saloon with a bullet in his chest, usually for cheating in a card game. St. Louis was a tough town!

Various Indian tribes lived in areas around St. Louis. Jean observed that there was a difference in language, religion, and culture, even though they had much in common physically. Most had large faces with high cheekbones, dark eyes, long, straight, black hair and reddish-brown skin with little facial hair.

INDIAN TRIBAL NAMES IN MIDDLE AMERICA

There are many different groups of Native Americans.
Large groups are called nations and nations are divided into tribes.
The Potawatomi are a part of the Algonquian Nation, along with the
Chippewa and the Ottawa. The Cahokia, Delaware, Fox, Huron,
Illinois, Iowa, Kansas Kaskaskia, Kickapoo, Miami, Michigamea,
Missouri, Muscatine, Omaha, Peoria, Sac, Shawnee, Sioux, and
Winnebago were among the tribes in the Midwest.

YES

WORK   TOGETHER

To be able to communicate with each other and with traders, the Indians devised a simple understandable sign language. It enabled them to "talk" with each other. In time, Jean understood much of the sign language and tried to learn as many of the Indian dialects as he could. One day a tall stranger came into the trading post. Having been out in the woods for months, he was dirty and ragged looking. "Know where I can get some home cookin', a tub of hot water, and a place to put my head tonight?" he asked. "I'd like to be with the human race again, at least for a while. My name is Arne." He put out his big, rough, dirty hand for Jean to shake.

Jean made a couple of suggestions and Arne was out the door. Two days later Arne strolled back into the post and blustered, "I don't like to wait too long between trips, so I'm takin' off. Thank you for your help, and I will see you next time. "Say," he hesitated, "if you ever get tired of the trading post and want to join me, I could use the help."

Over the next month, Jean began to mull over the idea of learning how to trap and hunt and going into uncharted wilderness with Arne. After deliberating the issue and finally making up his mind to go, he used this time productively. He had a friend teach him how to use a bow and arrow and a rifle. Now he was looking forward to trying his skill at trapping. He felt he could not pass up this opportunity to broaden his exposure to adventure.

So when Arne walked back into the trading post two months later, Jean's first words were, "Where do I sign up to go with you?"

Arne was taken aback. "Are you sure?" he questioned. "I want you to know what you are getting into. It is dangerous out there! You have to be alert 24 hours a day. There may be animal attacks, snake bites, unfriendly Indians, and untold other problems. How does that sound to you?"

"I want to go," Jean insisted.

Although Henri hated to loose Jean as his valued employee, he helped Jean get outfitted for his life as a trapper. The trading post carried everything he needed for the trip. He bought a loose-fitting, buckskin hunting shirt that had pockets for carrying food and mittens. It had leather fringe that ran across the shoulders and down the outside of the arm of the shirt. Jean was told these leather strips were used not only for decoration, but to keep rain from seeping through the seams. The fringe could be cut off and used to repair moccasins. The best moccasins were made of moose hide. The smoke from many fires made the hide extra tough footwear. Jean also bought buckskin pants that ended at the knees, which were convenient for wading in the water to set beaver traps. Leggings were worn below the knees for warmth when it was cold.

Slung across his chest by a strap, Jean slipped a buckskin bag holding gunpowder, a chunk of lead, and a mold to make bullets for his new muzzle-loading rifle. A pouch hung from his belt carrying needles, thread, fishhooks, a tin cup and spoon, a flint, and some dried buffalo meat called jerky to eat. He also packed beaver "medicine," a mixture of beaver glands and wild herbs to spread on a trap to attract an animal. Into his belt he thrust a long hunting knife. Jean topped off his outfit with a raccoon-skin cap with its striped tail flipped around his ear.

"Jean, let me look at you. You are one good-looking trapper! I want you to know that I will miss you, but this will be good for you."

Henri thought the experience Jean would gain as a trapper would make him even more valuable when he returned to work at the trading post.

Jean was eager to get going.

The morning Jean and Arne set out was cold and gray. It didn't take Jean long to understand why Arne was an extraordinary woodsman. He knew the rich hunting grounds and connecting waters that flowed from one stream into another, and he loved to share his knowledge.

"Are we out mostly for beaver pelts?" asked Jean.

"Except for food, that is all we are going to trap," Arne answered. "Let me tell you about beavers," Arne went on. "They weigh between 30 to 40 pounds and can live 10 years. They have a large, flat tail, rich fur, and sharp teeth that continue to grow as long as they live. Beavers use their teeth to cut down trees to build their homes in rivers and streams, called beaver dams. When you see the flat track of the beaver's tail in mud and bits of green wood floating on the water, you know a beaver is nearby."

Arne and Jean were successful in trapping a number of prize beavers. Jean watched as Arne flipped a dead beaver over, made a slit down the middle of the animal's belly, emptied the innards, removed the skin, folded it into itself, and packed it in the carrying pouch.

They walked for days in swamps with water up to their knees or higher, pushed through thickets and climbed slippery rocks. Despite these hardships, Jean was attracted to this kind of life: the beauty of the wilderness, the fresh fragrances of the woods, the thrill of discovery, the freedom, the peacefulness. He felt at home in the woods. He thought the nights would be quiet, but they were not. There were always whispering sounds in the grass and strange noises in the air. He imagined animal eyes glowing near his body. When sleep came, he often awoke, chilled by the sounds of deer blowing and stomping, raccoons chittering, and coyotes barking. He was scared, but it was exciting.

After ten days in the woods, the two men had trapped all they could carry, and they returned to St. Louis, exhausted and filthy, but rich in furs.

Arne and Jean walked into the trading post to show Henri their pelts.

"Good work, boys. I can give you a tidy sum of money for these furs. By the way, Jean, we are busier than ever. Can you come in to work tomorrow?"

"I think I can clean up by then, Henri," Jean responded with a smile.

CHAPTER 5

NEW EXPERIENCES

As Jean approached his room at Etta Jones' house, he saw a note on his door. "Come see me, Jean, when you get back." When he found Etta, he learned that her sister was moving to St. Louis.

"I'm not sure when she will be here, but I wanted to let you know that I may need your room on short notice," Etta said. Disappointed, Jean now had to be on the lookout for a new place to live.

When Jean returned to work, he learned the three Schulze brothers, regulars at the trading post, were building a log home to sell. Jean asked them if they could use his help on the house. He had an idea that might serve both him and the brothers.

"I will help you finish the house you are building in my free time from the trading post," he said. "In exchange, I could live in the log house until you sell it."

The brothers agreed that this was a good idea, so Jean met them at the property the next day. He discovered there was an art to building a log home. The solid rock foundation running the length and width of the house had already been laid, and the trees were downed, trimmed and notched to fit into one another at the corners of the house, creating the walls. The stone chimney was in place and the plank roof was ready to apply.

The process took about three months.

Once the roof was finished, the brothers were happy to have Jean move into the house where they could work together on the interior. Again the trading post carried everything they needed: saws, axes, wedges, and mauls. Jean enjoyed the physical labor after being at the post all day and the idea of living in a house that he helped build.

Jean liked St. Louis. Etta Jones, his former landlady, had taken an interest in him. He often fixed things at her house and ran errands for her. Etta knew that Jean had no family in St. Louis and that the boatmen who came with him to St. Louis had returned to New Orleans. Etta asked Mary, her married daughter, who lived in town, if she would include Jean in some family dinners.

Jean eagerly accepted those invitations and took his fiddle to entertain Mary, her husband Elmer, and their children Jonathan and Maggie. Maggie, just 10, had blond ringlets that curled around her ears, big blue eyes, and a wide smile. Jonathan, though two years younger, was almost as tall as his sister. They were both open and friendly and looked forward to Jean's visits. As time went on, Jean became a regular at Mary and Elmer's Sunday evening table.

Jonathan and Maggie were enchanted with Jean's stories. He told them about his homeland, and the sailors he had met who traveled all over the world. He drew pictures of the ships he worked on and the huge fish he had seen. Some nights he taught them to play the fiddle, other nights he helped them with their schoolwork. Jean was grateful this family accepted and included him. He viewed Jonathan and Maggie much like a younger brother and sister.

Whooping cough was a serious and sometimes fatal disease at that time. So one day when Maggie came home with a bad cough and high fever, the doctor confirmed the family's fear. Maggie had whooping cough. Over the next few weeks, the little girl's racking coughs became worse. She found it difficult to eat and became dangerously weak.

During this time, Jean stopped by Maggie's house every day on his way from work. He took her small gifts from the trading post; glass beads, a fur bracelet, colorful ribbons and always his fiddle to play. His music seemed to quiet her. As she became more ill, he would just sit by Maggie's bed, hold her hand, and sing to her. He studied her pretty face which had lost its healthy glow and listened to her panting for air. Her spirit was slipping quietly away. He was frightened he was going to lose her.

One day at work, a family friend came to tell Jean that Maggie died a few hours earlier. She was gone! He could not believe she died before he had a chance to say goodbye.

Jean was heartbroken. He had never experienced the death of someone so young and dear to him. Why was such a beautiful, little girl left to suffer and die? He could not understand. He immediately went to the house to be with Etta, Mary, Elmer, and Jonathan. Jean could not remember ever having been so sad.

"Could you play your fiddle at her grave?" Mary asked Jean. So with tears streaming down his face, Jean played Maggie's favorite songs as they lowered the small, white casket into the ground.

Mary continued to ask Jean to come to family dinners, and he did for awhile, but he missed Maggie so much that it was hard for him. Too many things in town reminded him of Maggie.

Jean wasn't enjoying his job at the trading post anymore. Nothing seemed to interest him or make him happy. Henri could see the change in Jean. He was expecting Jean to make a decision to leave St. Louis. Henri was right.

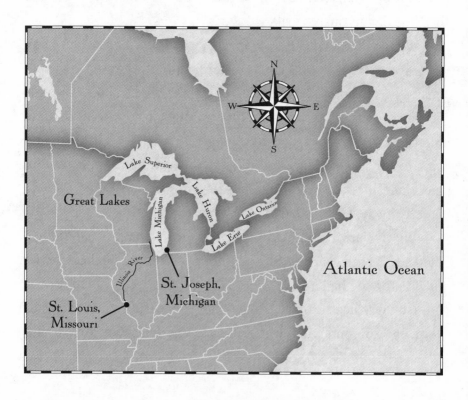

I have got to make some adjustments in my life, Jean thought, but what and how? I am 22 years old, and it is time for me to move on. I would like to see for myself the rich hunting grounds that I hear about from the people who come here.

He didn't know what was north of St. Louis although he did know that there were waterways that led to the Atlantic Ocean. It was a vast territory and he was sure he could not strike out by himself. He needed to find someone who could teach him how to survive in the untamed country.

There was a Potawatomi Indian from the St. Joseph Village up north who came to the trading post every six months. He had just arrived as Jean was contemplating his move. His name was Red Cloud. He was tall, with a broad, flat face and high cheekbones. His nose had a slight hook to it. Two thick braids fell forward over his strong muscular shoulders. A cluster of drooping eagle feathers were attached to the back of the colorful band that circled his head. He wore a deerskin shirt, leggings, and dark brown ankle-high moccasins. Around his neck, he wore multi-colored strands of beads mixed with small animal bones. Large silver hoops hung from pierced ears. Red Cloud was impressive!

When Red Cloud finished trading his furs for the supplies needed at home, Jean nervously asked him, "Red Cloud, I would like to go to St. Joseph with you. I long to see the rivers, lakes, meet the people I know in name only, and live for awhile the life you live. Would that be possible?"

Red Cloud with his forearms folded across his chest, eyed Jean with a strong steady, gaze before slowly asking him, "Do you hunt? Do you know the woods? Do you know fire power? Can you survive on nothing? If you can answer yes to those questions, then I will take you."

"I honestly think I can answer yes to those questions, Red Cloud."

Red Cloud nodded slowly. "When will you be ready?"

Jean could think of no one he would rather have lead him to his next series of adventures.

CHAPTER 6

NORTH COUNTRY

The morning of departure dawned clear and bright. The sun was making its way up into the sky when the two settled themselves into Red Cloud's 12-foot birch-bark canoe.

Red Cloud was an agreeable companion. He spoke only when necessary; he did not seem unhappy or dissatisfied, just quiet. He knew the campsites to select for their protection from the wind and wild predators, as well as unfriendly humans. He was a man of unusual energy, ability, and courage.

As they began their paddle up the Mississippi River, north of St. Louis, they encountered nature in all of its majesty. Following them on their journey were hundreds of birds of every description. Bald eagles, osprey, falcons, and hawks cruised over the river,

INDIAN BIRCH-BARK CANOE

This kind of boat, invented by the Indians, was sturdy and lightweight. It was constructed from the rind of a birch tree that grew in the north woods. It was pointed at both ends and propelled by paddles.

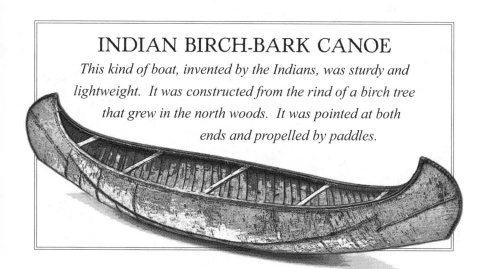

or perched in trees. Large fish arched and splashed in the water. Limestone rock towered high on each side of the river.

Leaving the Mississippi River, they turned northeast up the Illinois River, a 273-mile trek. On calm days, they could average 50 miles a day. If the wind was at their back, they went faster. However, headwinds generally kept them on shore because the bark canoe could be damaged. The trip took them over a week before coming to the Des Plaines River. They traveled days until the river became too muddy to paddle, Red Cloud announced, "We are at Mud Lake, we walk and carry now."

Jean and Red Cloud anchored the canoe on shore, strapped the bundles they were hauling onto their backs, and started across muddy soil. After putting their cargo on dry land, they returned to

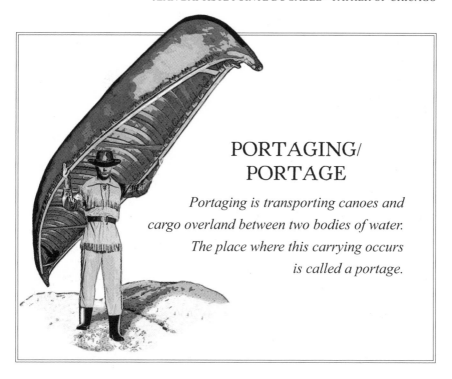

PORTAGING/ PORTAGE

Portaging is transporting canoes and cargo overland between two bodies of water. The place where this carrying occurs is called a portage.

pick up the canoe and carried it about four miles to the headwater of the next river which flowed into a huge body of water called Lake Michigan. This process is called portaging, carrying cargo and boat across land to the next body of water.

Dusk was settling in as they finished carrying their last load of belongings.

"Too much wind on the big lake. It is not wise to start out. We will stay here tonight and wait to see if tomorrow is good for travel." said Red Cloud.

Jean took time to view the land around him. He was fascinated. He had seen nothing comparable to the woods, wild flowers, fertile soil, and prairies. It looked like a hunter's paradise to Jean with an abundance of game and water in which to fish. He wanted to spend more time here. He set in his mind that he would return to this spot because he had a premonition of good fortune.

CHICAGO

Because there was no Indian written language at the time of du Sable,
words were spelled as they sounded – Checagou – Eschikagou.

"This is such a remarkable place. Is there a name for it?" asked Jean.

"We call it "C H E C A G O U," answered Red Cloud. "What does that mean?" asked Jean.

"It means strong, powerful," said Red Cloud

"Why hasn't someone settled here?" Jean asked Red Cloud.

"For years, Indians of many tribes fought here until my people, the Potawatomi Indians, drove them away and secured the area," Red Cloud explained.

Jean and Red Cloud built a fire and cooked the fish they caught in the river. A friendship had developed between the two. This was a night to review some of the hardships and dangers they encountered during their voyage. Once they avoided the wrath of a charging mother black bear and her cub; another time they barely escaped a hostile group of Indians. And there was the time when Jean tipped over the canoe in some rushing falls, almost drowning both of them. Their near disasters seemed too many to recount. It was a good night to laugh, joke, and tease one another.

The next morning at sunrise, they picked up their supplies and carried them to the shoreline of Lake Michigan, a huge body of water looking like an ocean to Jean. They set forth paddling eastward close to the southern shore of the lake until they reached the mouth of the St. Joseph River. They canoed up the St. Joseph River toward the village of St. Joseph.

How are the Potawatomi Indians going to respond to me? Jean wondered. It is one thing that I feel comfortable with Red Cloud. It may be another in this village of Potawatomi Indians I haven't met. Have they seen a white man before? I am sure they have not seen a man with my dark-colored skin. Will that make a difference to them? Jean was asking himself these things before they approached the village.

CHAPTER 7

ST. JOSEPH SETTLEMENT

At long last, Jean and Red Cloud saw the dim outline of the shore and the site of their destination on the St. Joseph River. "We are here," said Red Cloud. Jean was relieved to see the end of the long journey, but he was nervous about walking into the village that was strange to him. The two men anchored and unloaded the canoe and proceeded through the trees toward the settlement. As they walked, dogs barked and children ran from behind a thick stand of trees to see who was coming. Several women and old men followed the children. Shouts of greeting rang out as soon as they recognized Red Cloud. Jean followed his Indian friend. No one directly acknowledged Jean, but he was aware of the many faces staring at him with curiosity. He was obviously not an Indian.

To make a good impression, Jean thought to bring with him multi-colored beads, braided fabric, and hair ornaments to distribute as gifts. As he moved through the group that gathered, he dropped these colorful items into the hands of the children. Their squeals of joy pleased him and made him feel more at ease.

The St. Joseph campsite was large and sprawling. Beautiful lodges made of birch-bark were scattered among the pines. There was a forest stream where children were swimming. Women were busy over their cooking fires and several old men, bare to

the waist, sat at the entrances to their lodges, sharpening arrow tips in the sunshine.

Jean walked to where several children were playing a game. They were squatting in a wide circle throwing small stones into the middle and trying to hit a larger rock. He made hand motions asking if he could join them. They giggled and showed him what to do. As they played together and the children became more comfortable with Jean, a few of them ran their fingers across his hand and arms to see if the color of his skin would rub off. They took turns touching his curly hair because theirs was straight. After this first curious encounter, no one was concerned about the dark color of Jean's skin.

Without warning, the camp burst into wild shouts and screams. The children jumped up and ran toward some returning hunters. Young Indian men marched into the middle of the campsite and dropped from their shoulders the deer they had killed. A feast was on the way! Swiftly the women skinned the animals and began to prepare the meal. They increased the size of the fire and added the meat, water, roots, and berries to the kettles. In time the savory fragrance of the boiling meal drew everyone close to the cooks. When the food was ready, the men settled themselves in a circle closest to the fire. The women sat behind the men and the children ate last feasting on what was left.

After they all had eaten, Red Cloud took Jean by the elbow, saying, "The leaders gather at the council lodge. They want to meet with you. We will go now."

Red Cloud and Jean pressed through a deerskin entryway into a lodge that was spacious, clean and well-ventilated, even with a fire burning inside. The Indian men sat silently in a circle around the fire. They turned to the left and walked behind the group to the back of the lodge where Jean and Red Cloud were motioned to join. The Indians sat cross-legged with eagle feathers stuck in their hair, their bodies wrapped in colorful blankets. The faces were illuminated by the light of the flickering fire. The Indian of the highest rank sat furthest from the opening.

"My name is Chief Wabasi," he introduced himself, "We know from Red Cloud that your name is Jean Baptiste Pointe du Sable. We welcome you. Please share with us the sacred pipe to honor your visit before you tell us why you have come."

Jean was instantly impressed with Chief Wabasi. He looked to be about 45 years of age. His muscular body sat erect. His long, jet black hair parted in the middle hung below his shoulders draping a narrow face that held dark piercing eyes. His voice was soft but deep.

Chief Wabasi picked up the calumet, a stone bowl pipe adorned with long feathers. He carefully put a mixture of tobacco and various aromatic herbs into the bowl, lit it, and put it to his lips. He drew in and slowly blew out a long puff of smoke that symbolized a breath of prayer. The pipe was passed from one to another until it came to Jean who copied what the others had done then passed it back to Chief Wabasi.

"Now tell us about yourself, du Sable," the chief said.

"Thank you, Chief Wabasi, it is a privilege to be here."

With the help of Red Cloud on the journey, Jean learned enough of the language of the Potawatomi to speak with some fluency. It was relatively easy for him to tell those assembled about his background and his reasons for wanting to come and stay with them for awhile.

"In my work at the trading post in St. Louis, I met Indians from many tribes," Jean said. "I admired them, but, their lives seemed a mystery to me. I had been told that in this land where you live, hunting and trapping is the most beautiful and bountiful. I asked Red Cloud if I could come here and see for myself."

"You are welcome, but if you will excuse us, we need to talk among ourselves now," said the chief.

Jean rose to his feet, bowed, and walked out of the lodge the way he had entered. Once outside, he let out a deep breath. He had no idea what their decision about him would be. Where would he go if they did not let him stay? Nervously, he paced back and forth until Red Cloud appeared.

Red Cloud greeted Jean with a smile. "They like the way you take time to play with the children, talk to the women, and listen to the stories of the elders. We will find a place for you."

Jean returned the smile, saying, "Please tell your brothers that I thank them from the bottom of my heart."

As the sun grew low in the sky, Jean and Red Cloud were summoned to the council lodge to hear of Red Cloud's adventures since he had been away. The Indians also took turns telling Red Cloud of events that occurred during his absence.

Red Cloud had a wife, so Jean knew that he would not stay with him when it was time to retire. Red Cloud led Jean to a small dome-shaped lodge covered with birch-bark away from the close circle of bigger lodges. When Jean pulled back the deer-hide flap of the entrance, he found a large buffalo robe for his bed. Before he sank his tired body down on the soft, luxurious skin, Jean extended his hand and said, "Thank you, Red Cloud, for all you have done for me. I will repay your kindness."

CHAPTER 8

THE POTAWATOMI: KEEPERS OF THE FIRE

For the next few days, Jean observed the routine of the Indian men. Before the sun lifted in the eastern sky, the older men followed by the younger ones, went to the lake to bathe. This was a daily ritual, even in the winter, to keep their bodies clean and strong so they could endure cold and discomfort. On certain days after bathing, several men went to the sweat lodge. This structure was shaped like the rounded upper half of a ball. Inside was a small pit that held heated rocks that had been moved into the lodge from the fire hearth outside of the east-facing entrance. They poured water on the rocks. The resulting steam rose to purify the body and soul and to carry messages of petition and gratitude to the Creator. Jean was honored to be invited to join in these cleansing rituals.

Later the council met to discuss possible attacks and raids by hostile Indian tribes. The Potawatomi had been chased out of lands further to the east by the warring Iroquois Indians, and they would fight any who tried to move them again. Not long after Jean had arrived, he went on some of their hunting expeditions for deer, moose and bear. Although most of the Indians treated him in a friendly manner, not all the Indians at camp approved of his living with them on any kind of a permanent basis. Some felt he was not contributing enough for what he was receiving, though Jean was trying to broaden his knowledge and do what was expected of him.

One day, as Jean was walking in the woods, a young woman moved along the open path carrying a water jug on her shoulder. Their eyes met for an instant and then she lowered her face, quickened her pace, and brushed past him. He stood staring after her, taking in her beauty as she continued on her way. Jean wondered who she was. Up to this point he had not paid much attention to the women of the tribe, but this one caught his eye. Her silky, black hair lay in one large braid that cascaded down her back. She was as beautiful as any young woman he had ever seen. She walked with a natural grace and dignity of which she seemed unaware. At that quick glance, it was hard for him to determine her age. He knew many of the young women of the tribe were already spoken for or even had babies.

After that encounter, Jean began to look for her among the women at the campsite. In doing so, he observed all the work the women did in the camp. It was the women who planted the crops and tended to them, scraped and tanned the animal hides, built the fires, and cooked the food. It was the women who made the clothing and decorated it with paints, porcupine quillwork, feathers, ribbons, and glass beads. They cared for the children and the elders. Their work was essential and highly valued.

The more Jean searched for the young woman, the more he grew interested in meeting her. Finally, with some nervousness, he sought out Red Cloud's help. "There is a maiden here that I would like to know," he said to his friend. "Tell me if she is already married. If not, how can I approach her?"

Red Cloud asked Jean to point the woman out to him. Later that night Jean saw her around the campfire. "There she is," he whispered.

"You choose well," Red Cloud told him. "Her name is Kittahawa. She is part of the chief's family. I will ask her brother if she is free to meet you." With that, Red Cloud slipped away.

Soon he returned with good news. "She belongs to no one," Red Cloud informed Jean. "If you want, I will ask Half Day, her brother, to get permission from her parents for you." Before the evening ended, Red Cloud came to Jean and said, "They have agreed that you may introduce yourself to her."

That night Jean was alert for the opportunity to meet with Kittahawa as he waited near the spot where he thought she would pass, hoping for a smile or an exchange of words. When that didn't happen, he positioned himself the next morning near her lodge and when she came out, he spoke: "Kittahawa, my name is Jean Baptiste Pointe du Sable. I am hoping that you could make some time for us to take a walk. Is that possible?"

Her eyes were warm and bright as she nodded and smiled, "Yes, after I finish my work."

Later in the day Jean and Kittahawa met. On their walk Jean said, "You have such a pretty name, tell me who gave it to you."

"My father named me Kittahawa, but I have a second name," she said. "My second name is Catherine. Years ago, Jesuit missionary priests were here and brought us their religious teaching and baptized me Catherine. That is why I have two names."

"Which do you like?" Jean asked her.

"I like both. You choose what you like," she answered shyly.

"I like both too, but Catherine is a saint's name." said Jean, "I think it suits you. May I call you Catherine?"

"Yes," she smiled.

After that first meeting, they were together as much as their responsibilities would allow. Jean knew he wanted to spend the rest of his life with her. It was obvious to others, including her parents, that Jean was in love with Catherine. In time he would talk with Chief Wabasi, Catherine's grandfather, about Catherine and his plans for leaving the village.

In the meantime, Jean lived through his first Michigan winter, one that the Indians told him was more brutal than most. He was surprised how the snowshoes that Catherine made for him could help a traveler walk on top of the snow. The dogsled was used for longer trips.

Jean thought about what he had observed and learned from living with the Potawatomi. He found their life interesting. He admired how well they worked together for the common well-being of the tribe. The Indians loved their children who were treated gently yet firmly. They let the children be children until they reached a certain age. When the boys were about eight years old, the fathers and the uncles taught them how to fish, use bows and arrows, and trap small animals. As they got older, they were taught how to follow the tracks of man and animal, how to tell the weather, and how to use a tomahawk. At 15, if they demonstrated ability, they were old enough to accompany the warriors to defend their land

and people. At ages eight and ten, the mothers were teaching their daughters to sew, plant, harvest, cook, and take care of younger siblings.

Storytelling was recreation for everyone. This was the important job of the elders who knew how to capture the listener's attention. "I want you to know what happened a long, long time ago. You must keep these stories and tell them to your children and their children," the storyteller would begin. The elders educated the audience about the importance of carrying on their cultural traditions through dances, songs, chants, and how to live respectable and spiritual lives.

It was spring now and Jean was eager to explore other areas of this north country. He realized he would need the chief's help with his important connections and influence with Indian trappers throughout the area. Jean also knew that he brought unique new thinking to them. In St. Louis, he had dealt with Indians of various tribes as well as the French, Spanish, and English traders.

"Chief Wabasi, being with you and your people has taught me so much. I appreciate your generous hospitality and patience," Jean said. "It is as if I have acquired a new set of relatives. But I see a future that takes me away from my friends here. I will explore, learn, come back with what I know, and hopefully, expand our horizons."

"It is good that you want to do this, Jean. We have connections in Peoria, among other places. We will help you get ready for your journey," replied the Chief.

"Thank you. I plan to be leaving in the next few days," answered Jean.

Jean traveled to Peoria where a band of Potawatomi lived. He stayed there long enough to develop some land for farming.

While in Peoria, he met people traveling up the Illinois River with destinations to the Great Lakes. Jean told them of the portage near the Des Plaines River and how they could move on to Lake Michigan. The more Jean told travelers about the portage, the more he saw a potential for him to live there – do his trapping, fishing, and trading. He could guide travelers through the area. Jean saw a need not being met and he decided to be the person to fill it.

"Jean, you surprise us with your return," Chief Wabasi greeted him. Are you staying for awhile?"

"Chief Wabasi, I am excited about an idea and I would like to share it with you. Before I do though, I want you to know I will need your assistance," Jean said.

"Explain it to me, Jean," said the chief.

"When I first came here, I told you I found a place where I could trap, hunt, fish, and live. Now I see a bigger potential there. I would like to set up a structure where I could live and help those travelers moving from north to south and back at the portage. According to the needs of the travelers, I would develop my own trading post. Our Indian friends from the surrounding areas could bring their pelts to me and I would have the items they need to better their lives. It would be good for your people here because they would not have to travel so far for their trading," explained Jean.

"Your idea sounds interesting, Jean, We will meet at council tonight and you can tell our brothers," said the chief.

Red Cloud was the next person Jean saw upon his return.

"Jean," greeted Red Cloud," Did you come back to get the fiddle that you left in my care while you were gone?"

"I did, Red Cloud, but also to see you. I have missed you, my friend."

Jean and Red Cloud walked toward the river as Jean told Red Cloud of his plans.

"I like it. I will help you," said Red Cloud.

Everyone was glad to see Jean again as he passed gifts to the men, women, and children.

In the council meeting, the chief asked Jean to tell those who gathered what he wanted to do and the kind of help he needed from them.

"I would like to build a house on the land by the big lake and the river, near the portage and sometime put up another small building to keep the animal skins before I transport them. Could some men help me? On the property, I would have supplies, not only for you, but for trappers from the north, the west, and the south. Most importantly, when I am settled, I would like to have Catherine come with me as my wife." Jean nervously got all of his petitions out. There was silence.

Chief Wabasi said nothing at first, but he felt that Jean would be a good provider for Catherine. Economic security was important in marriage. The chief thought Catherine might like the new and different life, but he wasn't convinced of that yet.

Jean did not expect an immediate answer to his request to have Catherine as his wife, so he continued. "Red Cloud is good at buying supplies, but I have the experience of running a trading post. I know what supplies the trading post carries, where they get them, and how much they pay for them. I know animal skins, the good from the bad, and how much they are worth. Many different tribes and trappers frequented the post in St. Louis where I worked. I have dealt with them all."

The chief was thoughtful for a moment. "We have growing needs. Take Red Cloud to St. Louis with you, and we will compare the exchange of goods with what we are getting now."

Jean and Red Cloud readied themselves for the trip to St. Louis. Red Cloud agreed to camp overnight in Checagou. As it happened, they arrived at their first destination in the rain. Their clothes and baggage needed to dry before they moved on. This gave Jean time to look more carefully at the surrounding area. The property was forming in his imagination. He was picturing a house on the north side of the river near the lake.

"This is it, Red Cloud; I will be here someday, hopefully in the near future."

The trip to St Louis took about 12 days. When they arrived, they went to the trading post where Jean had worked. Henri Fontour, the owner, was behind the counter when they walked in.

Henri was so happy to see them that he was uncharacteristically expressive. "Jean, Jean, so good to see you," exclaimed Henri. He grabbed Jean's hand with both of his. "You have come back to be with us?"

"No, Henri, I am afraid not," said Jean, "I am living with the Potawatomi in St. Joseph. My friend and I are here to trade and buy supplies. I trust you to give us the best deal that you can."

"Let me see what you have, Jean," said Henri. Red Cloud and Jean emptied the boat of their pelts and laid them out for Henri. They decided on a price that pleased both Henri and Jean.

"It looks like there is more growth and activity here in St. Louis since I left, Henri," Jean commented.

"Yes, we have new people coming all the time. My business is growing. If you come back, I could definitely use you."

"Thank you, Henri, I must decline your kind invitation. But I am sure I will be back to see you many times again." Jean said.

Jean and Red Cloud gathered up their supplies, said goodbye, and set out for home. The men again stopped in Checagou for Jean to dream before returning to St. Joseph." Yes, this is the place, Red Cloud," stated Jean.

Great excitement spread throughout the camp when they arrived back in St. Joseph. There were trinkets for the children, ribbon and beads for the women, and knives and guns for the men. Jean packed extra gifts for Catherine, and he brought Catherine's father a gun and a blanket.

"How did the people in St. Louis like the pelts you took them, Jean?" Chief Wabasi asked when they had a chance to talk.

"My friend, Henri, owner of the trading post, said the pelts from this part of the country are among the best he has ever seen. He wants us back as often as we can get there," Jean answered.

"That is good and you have done well trading for what we need," said Chief Wabasi.

Over the next several months, Jean and Red Cloud made other successful trading trips that pleased Chief Wabasi.

"You have proven yourself to be worthy of our consideration to help start your project in the Checagou area. I will call council to discuss the matter," Chief Wabasi said.

CHAPTER 9

A NEW BEGINNING

An hour passed, though it seemed much longer to Jean before the chief emerged from the council tent.

"Jean du Sable," the chief began, "the brothers like your idea of developing the area near the portage. When the ice is out of the lakes, I will send some men with you to the location called Checagou to help you build a house. When that is done, we will contact our Potawatomi brothers in Peoria and other places nearby and ask them to bring their best furs to you. If you prove yourself worthy of their trust, you may return to our village and take Catherine with you as your wife. If our Indian friends feel you do not trade well or are not honest with them, then Catherine will stay with us, and we will no longer use your services.

Jean understood he needed to prove himself and appreciated the confidence the chief and others had in him. He was determined to do well.

Several times during the winter, Jean traveled the 90 miles by dog sled to Checagou to decide where he would build his home. In his mind, he could see the house on the hilltop with a commanding view overlooking both the river and the lake. He envisioned a garden where they would grow food for their table. He would have animals, a barn and a workshop. He was eager to start. Let us get this winter over, he thought to himself.

Shortly after the ice melted on the lake, and spring arrived, seven Indians from St. Joseph joined Jean in the Checagou area to cut down trees and begin construction of his log home, a home like the ones he and the Schulze brothers built in St. Louis. All summer they worked, and before the cold breezes of winter set in, the house was finished enough for Jean to move in. He started to work on his plans for the trading post.

Chief Wasabi made good on his promise to send business to Jean. The reports of Jean's performance were favorable.

Upon returning to St. Joseph in the spring, Jean again approached Chief Wabasi about marrying Catherine.

"I am pleased with you, Jean," Chief Wabasi said. "You have done well for us. You may take Catherine with you. We will prepare a feast for the two of you on the day of the full moon."

The next two weeks passed slowly for Jean and Catherine. Eagerly and happily, the women of the village were getting ready for the festivities, since the Indians never missed a chance to celebrate an event. Finally, the happy day arrived, and what a day it was! The air was crisp and the sun shown brightly on the village. The children were excited as the women rushed preparing the feast. All were dressed in their finest clothes. Chief Wabasi appeared from his lodge in his buckskins and a huge feathered headdress. He walked with a sense of importance around the camp calling people to the celebration.

Jean's friends had taken special care in preparing him for the wedding. They tied eagle feathers in his hair, and dressed him in new deerskin and beaded moccasins. A shirt, decorated with porcupine quills and bear teeth, was pulled over his head. Around his arms and legs they fastened rattles that moved when he walked. They were proud of the way Jean looked and never had Jean felt so handsome.

The air was alive with expectation. A crowd assembled in the center of the camp. They cheered when they saw Catherine appear from her family lodge. She wore a long white deerskin dress that draped from her shoulders in graceful folds. Soft feathers and colorful beads were woven into her silken, black hair that spilled down her back. Holding onto the arm of her father, Catherine walked slowly to where her grandfather stood.

When she reached the center of the camp, Chief Wabasi took Catherine's hand from her father and walked her around the campfire and through the crowd of family and friends. He led her back to stand next to Jean who smiled at her lovingly. The chief draped a beautiful, large, white blanket around the shoulders of the couple. The blanket signified that the couple was now one and would stay together forever. Jean held Catherine's hand and turned toward the east as they were directed. Chief Wabasi stood before the couple and recited the ancient four directions of Potawatomi teachings.

"East is the direction of the yellow sun," he said, "meaning spring, infancy, optimism, and the beginning of all good things to come."

The chief next led the couple to face south and said, "South is the color black, the season of summer, young adulthood, and change."

Directing the couple to the west, the chief said, "West is the color of the setting sun, red, autumn, middle age, and wise teachers. At death, we pass through to the great mystery."

Finally, Chief Wabasi led the couple to face north and said, "North is the color white like the snow and the hair of the elders. We must respect the cleansings that come from this direction. It is the direction of wisdom from which the great healer, Muko the bear, comes."

The chief stepped back and said to the couple as well as to those assembled, "Jean and Catherine, you have become one. The young, the middle, and the elders pass on to you our teachings for a life together of love and blessings."

The words that the chief pronounced joined them in the union of man and wife. The formality of the ceremony was lightened when the group burst into chanting, singing, drumming, and dancing. Jean and Catherine led the festivities by being the first to dance around the fire. Then the adults and children chimed in and danced through the night.

At the end of that special day, Jean led Catherine to the lodge that had been decorated by Catherine's mother, aunts, and girlfriends with colorful blankets and presents of wild rice and flowers, their home until they moved to Checagou.

The festivities continued for days with games, races, music, food, and dancing. The children played until they collapsed, exhausted. The old people felt young again. When the celebrating died down and the tired people slowly returned to their daily chores, Jean looked forward to taking Catherine to the home he had waiting for her.

He could not help but look back on his life since he left Santo Domingo at age 18. He never could have imagined himself in an Indian village, marrying Catherine, the woman he loved. How he wished his parents could know how happy he was! He was wearing the medal and chain his Mother had given him when he left home.

CHAPTER 10

HOME

The day arrived when Jean and Catherine would leave St. Joseph to go to their new home in Checagou. Catherine's relatives and friends had packed and put food and bundles of clothing into the canoe. The children from the village gathered around Catherine all wanting her attention. "No, No," they begged, trying to hold on to her, for they all loved Catherine and did not want her to leave.

"I will be back to see you," she promised. Her friends circled her and gave her hugs. Her mother and father walked with her down to where the canoe was tied. As she stepped into the canoe Catherine tried to be brave, but it was hard. She settled herself on the seat in the front of the canoe, with her back to those assembled on the banks of the river, her head hung low. Jean said his goodbyes, waved and pushed off into the river. The children followed as far as they could, their cries of "Don't leave us!" ringing in her ears, as Catherine and Jean moved out into the water. Not a word was spoken between the two of them. Catherine felt sick to her stomach as she swallowed her sobs. She was already homesick for her family and friends.

Jean looked at the hunched-over figure of his new bride in front of him. He understood her sadness and tried to cheer her. "Catherine, your new home is beautiful," he said. "You will have your own garden, with a river and woods nearby. I think it will be perfect for us. We can come back and visit your family and friends, and they can come to see us."

Catherine did not respond. She is only 16, Jean thought. Maybe she is too young to move away from her family and all she knows. Maybe I made a mistake.

It was a long canoe trip, especially when your companion sits in silence. As the hours passed, Jean continued to talk to Catherine. "Your brothers came and worked all summer to build our house," he said with enthusiasm. "They cut the trees down. They put logs one on top of the other and then used small hand tools to chip away the rough wood. When the house was finished we had a great celebration. I know you will like this house, Catherine."

Catherine did not reply.

The last light of day was glistening on the lake when the long, quiet journey ended. Their canoe rounded the point, and the house came into view.

"There it is, Catherine. There is your new home – our home," Jean proudly stated. "We will live here, we will have children, and we will be happy."

Catherine raised her head and stared at the log house, but said nothing. She had never seen a house before! How was she supposed to live in a place that was so closed up? How could she hear the frogs, the crickets, and the birds? She KNEW she was not going to like it here.

Jean helped Catherine out of the canoe and picked up a pack to carry into the house. Catherine followed slowly with a sad face and slumped shoulders.

When they reached the house, Jean opened the door for Catherine to enter. Catherine stepped into a big room that had beautiful bearskins on the floor and more animal skins hanging on the walls. To the right, was a huge fireplace with a number of kettles hanging from rods that nearly covered one wall. To the left she saw a table and chairs, and the snowshoes Catherine made for Jean were hanging on the wall. Across the room was a doorway that led into another room where a bed was piled high with colorful blankets. All of this was too much of a change!

Catherine stood there staring and said, "I will sleep outside."

Though he was deeply troubled by this reaction, Jean knew that he needed to give Catherine time. She could not go back to her family as it would be a disgrace. For several days and nights Catherine worked, cooked, and slept outside alone. One day, when Jean had gone to catch fish for dinner, Catherine slowly entered the house and looked around more carefully. She walked into the bedroom. I can live in this house, she said to herself. I must, because Jean built it for me. It is best to accept it. Maybe this isn't such a bad place after all, she thought. Catherine moved into the house.

As hard as it was for her to adjust to the house, the loneliness that haunted her every day was much worse. She started feeding the squirrels, chipmunks, and birds. Sometimes a deer or two came close to the house. Catherine gave them each names and talked to them as friends.

"May I go with you today?" Catherine often asked Jean. On short day trips he enjoyed having her with him. Catherine would paddle the canoe and watch for game while Jean fished. Those days made Catherine happy.

The following fall, the two of them went to clear, shallow lakes and harvested the seed-bearing grass called wild rice. Jean stood in the front of the canoe and used a wooden pole to navigate through the rice beds. Catherine sat in the back, reached out with one hand, bent the stalks, and knocked the kernels into the boat with a stick. When the canoe was full, they returned home, spread the kernels on mats, and dried them. They stored the rice and cooked with it all year. Catherine had harvested wild rice all of her life. This activity made her feel close to her family.

Jean decided to add on to his property. The number of trappers and tradesmen who were traveling through on their way to the Mississippi River or to the Great Lakes was increasing. He wanted to expand to accommodate the needs of these people. He asked Chief Wabasi if he could again spare some men.

The chief was aware of Jean's success in dealing with the Indian trappers he sent. The St. Joseph Indians had to travel long distances to trade their pelts. If some of the families moved to Checagou, they could trap and trade their pelts to Jean. Chief Wabasi called a meeting of tribesmen to ask if there would be any families willing to move to Checagou and work with Jean and Catherine. About 20 agreed.

Soon, those families started to make their preparations. It was not difficult to relocate their family lodges. Their homes were made of tree saplings and birch-bark. The men drove the saplings into the ground in oval arches. The women tied the framework together and lay the birch-bark in layers over the curved shaped saplings, leaving an opening at the top. Deer hide covered the entrance.

That first winter was long for Catherine, but now that she had friends around her she was going to enjoy her new life.

CHAPTER 11

AN ADDITION

While the men put an addition on Jean and Catherine's house and built a barn, the women tilled the ground for a larger garden where they planted squash, pumpkin, corn, tobacco, and herbs. They also wove fishnets, made moccasins, cured animal skins, and sewed winter clothing.

Now that Catherine wasn't lonely, Jean was able to put more time into his business travels. His reputation was good among the Indians from surrounding areas. They brought their pelts to him in exchange for manufactured goods they wanted, such as iron tools, cooking utensils, blankets, and firearms.

When Jean returned from trips, he always brought something special for Catherine; a jeweled bracelet, a painting to hang on the wall, and silver candlesticks.

One day, when Jean arrived home from a trip, Catherine had some very exciting news for him. Catherine rushed to meet him when she heard him return. The first words out of her mouth were, "Jean, we are going to have a baby."

She kissed him, hugged him and danced around him. "I am so happy!" she said. "I waited to tell you before we told our friends. Now I can tell everybody. I can't wait to hold our baby in my arms. You will have to bring me fabrics, ribbons, beads, feathers, and everything I will need to make beautiful things for our baby. Jean," Catherine stopped and looking into his eyes said, "What do you think?"

"Of course, I'm happy, Catherine. That is what I said when we moved here, that we would have a family. Having a baby is what we both wanted. You will be a wonderful mother. It will be fun for us to plan for this child." Jean gave Catherine a reassuring hug. He was pleased to see Catherine so joyous.

Jean made the wooden cradleboard frame that Catherine would wear to carry her child. Catherine made the leather sack that was sewn onto the board. Soft rabbit fur lined the inside. She cut up colorful trade blankets to weave into the sack and attached beads and unusual feathers.

"Isn't it the most beautiful cradleboard you have ever seen, Jean?" she asked him repeatedly.

"Yes, Catherine," he always replied with a smile. "I have never seen anything more beautiful."

"Let's hang it on the wall so we can see it from every place in the house until the baby comes, and then I will wear it to keep the baby close to me."

CRADLEBOARD

A cradleboard was a piece of board about two feet long, one foot wide and one inch thick. An infant would be carried in a comfortable deerskin backpack attached to the board and strapped to the mother's back.

"Just tell me where you want me to hang it."

Jean walked around the house and held the cradleboard up to the wall in different places. "Here? Or here? Or over here?" he patiently asked.

"There!" Catherine finally said.

Jean hammered a peg in the wall just to the left of the fireplace, hung the board, and they sat down together to admire it.

Every day, as Catherine passed the cradleboard, she brushed her hand against it and grew more eager for the baby to come. As she waited, she continued to work in the gardens with her friends, gathering berries, mushrooms, corn, and squash. She skinned the small animals that were trapped near the house and prepared meals of goose, turkey, rabbit, and fish. Jean and his friends helped the women skin and prepare the larger animals – the moose, deer, and bear, and they helped dry the meat to preserve through the winter. Along with making Jean's shirts, leggings, moccasins, and snowshoes, Catherine was making baby clothes.

As the baby's arrival grew near, Jean stayed close to home. He used that time to plan more buildings. He wanted a separate building for a trading post where he could keep his tanned leathers, guns, knives, ammunitions, blankets, and trade cloth.

Finally, the time came for Catherine's mother and the tribe's midwife to come help deliver the baby. When the pains of labor started, Jean was called into the house, but not allowed into the bedroom with Catherine. Hours dragged by. Jean paced inside and outside of the house until he finally heard the cry of the newborn baby. He ran to the bedroom, but the midwife would not let him in. Something was not right.

"No, not yet," the midwife said.

"Is there something wrong?" Jean questioned in urgency.

The answer was cheerless and sober, "Yes."

Jean burst into the room that was full of shadow.

The baby had come, but was small and blue. It breathed just once or twice. The women worked hard to get the baby to breathe but to no avail. The baby died and lay lifeless in Catherine's mother's arms.

"Let me hold my baby," cried Catherine. Solemnly, her mother placed the quiet, lifeless baby in her arms. Jean knelt down next to his wife buried his head, next to Catherine's, and cried too. He was overcome with emotion. Now he knew how Mary and Elmer felt when their beloved Maggie died. A stillness settled in the house, but for the quiet sobs of Catherine.

Jean made a little wooden box, and he and Catherine buried the infant under the bedroom window. Jean did not travel for weeks afterward because he did not want to leave the grieving Catherine, who for days walked into the woods and cried for her baby.

One day while Jean was on the river fishing, Catherine built a fire in their yard – a big fire. She went into the house took the baby's cradleboard with all its decorations and trimmings off the wall, and threw it in the fire. The beads melted and feathers flew away as the cradleboard slowly disappeared. Catherine stood watching it burn with tears streaming down her face.

"There," she yelled, raising her face and arms to the heavens. "There! The Creator must be angry and did not want me to be happy."

Jean returned to find the extinguished bonfire, the missing cradleboard, and Catherine curled into a ball on the bed. He took her in his arms and promised her, "We will have other babies."

CHAPTER 12

CHANGING TIMES

Jean kept his promise, and Jean Jr., a healthy baby boy, was born in 1771. At first, Catherine was afraid to love the baby, afraid if she did, he too might die. But as time passed, she found Jean Jr. to be a constant delight. Jean was proud to have a son and looked forward to the time when the two of them could hunt and fish together.

Two years later, in 1773, another healthy baby was born, this time a girl named Susanne, after Jean's mother.

As Jean and Catherine's family expanded, several French Canadian trappers and their families moved to Checagou–Ouillemette, Pellitier among others. These people were disheartened by the British government who had gained control of Canada after France had lost its territory in the French and Indian War.

THE FRENCH AND INDIAN WAR

In the 1750s, France and Britain were fighting in Europe. Battles between the two countries erupted over territories in the New World. From 1754 to 1763, French soldiers and Indian warriors from many nations, including the Potawatomi, fought British soldiers and East Coast colonists over land in the New World. France lost the war along with all of its territory in Canada.

A large proportion of the Indians in the area also found the passing of control from the French to the English extremely unwelcome.

In the 1770s when Jean was doing business as a fur trader, he had not experienced any disruption by regional wars and changing governments. Yet as time went on, he learned that England's King George III was enforcing unjust taxes on the British colonial settlers. The 13 colonies were rebelling, wanting to be free from the King's tyrannical rule.

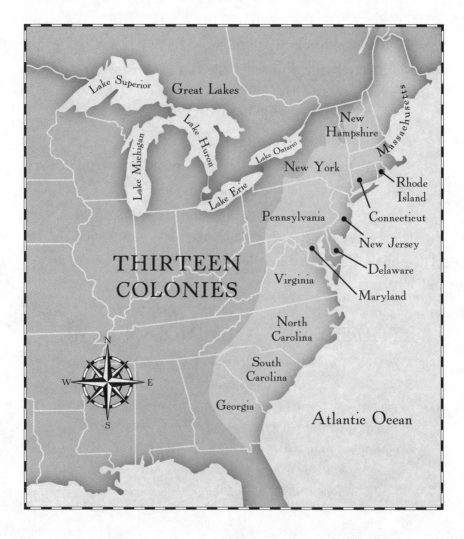

THE AMERICAN REVOLUTION
1775-1783

This war pitted the 13 British colonies along the eastern seaboard of America against the British government. The colonies successfully revolted and the United States of America was born. The Treaty of Paris was signed in 1783, ending British domination.

Leaders from the colonies met in Philadelphia, Pennsylvania to decide if they were going to cut ties with England. They chose George Washington to be their commander-in-chief. Furious at their rebellion, King George III sent troops from England to control the colonists. Skirmishes turned into battles and soon the colonies declared war.

The first shots of what was to be called the American Revolutionary War were fired in 1775.

One of Jean's important trading destinations was Detroit, Michigan, a British post. Although the fighting was east of Checagou, he did have to get along with people from both sides of the conflict. The British merchants didn't know if this black man from French Santo Domingo was on the side of the British, the colonists, or the Indians. But as long as du Sable brought furs of good quality to them, they remained business partners.

Jean continued to make trips down the Mississippi River to St. Louis. The old French villages, Vincennes, Kaskaskia, and Cahokia, that were on his route were now controlled by the British who kept an armed force in each town. Jean knew that the French settlers living there were not happy with the British occupation of their villages.

In 1779, Colonel George Rogers Clark, a hot-tempered, red-haired, young man from Kentucky, was ordered by the new American government to capture those villages until the Revolutionary War was won. Clark recruited men from Kentucky to join him in the move to the Mississippi River. Their goal was to take and hold this frontier for the newly formed American government. Clark's small army traveled by boat and marched by foot, enduring severe hardships of hunger and sickness, until they reached the destination. His men were outnumbered, but they surrounded the villages. Thanks to the element of surprise and some help from local citizens, Clark and his men were able to capture the three villages without a shot being fired. The British soldiers fled to Detroit.

Jean met Clark and his men in the village of Cahokia while on a trading trip to St. Louis. Jean could see that Clark's men were undernourished and exhausted. Clark told Jean that he was out of money to feed and clothe his men and had not received the pay due to him from the government to buy supplies.

"I have boats, food, medicine, and men who will help you at my post in Checagou," Jean told Clark.

"When we get there, we will gratefully accept any help you can give us," Clark said.

When Jean returned home, he told Catherine about meeting Colonel George Rodgers Clark. "One of these days we will be expecting Colonel Clark and his men. They need our help to continue their mission," Jean said. Catherine was used to helping people in need and would be prepared.

When Clark and his ragged, half-starved men appeared at the trading post in Checagou, Jean kept his bargain and housed, fed, and clothed them. Jean and Catherine sent them on their way with medicine and ammunition for their guns.

Information reached the British that Jean was collaborating with Clark and the revolutionaries. Because the Checagou portage was the perfect location for shipping and travel by traders, trappers, Indians, and soldiers, the British wanted control of Jean's property. They knew that the French sympathizer, du Sable, was working against them in their progress to capture and hold this frontier land. They saw Jean as a problem who needed to be removed from the Checagou portage.

CHAPTER 13

KIDNAPPED

Early one summer day in 1779, Jean, Catherine, and the children were clearing land for planting when they saw several men approach on horseback. The men were dressed in the red coats of the British soldiers. Jean stood erect, put down his hoe, and slowly walked to meet them.

"State your mission," Jean spoke to the man on the lead horse.

"Are you Jean Baptiste Pointe du Sable?" a stout man in the red coat replied in a curt British accent. His hard eyes were deep set in a proud, still face.

"I am, and your name?"

"My name is Lieutenant Thomas Bennett, and we have come by order of the British government to arrest you."

"On what charge?" Jean spoke angrily.

"On the grounds that you are carrying on treasonable trade with the enemy. You will come with us as we take control of this portage," Lieutenant Bennett ordered. "Our people are at the portage now." That said, Lieutenant Bennett sat tall on his horse and was silent.

Three men jumped from their horses and held Jean as one soldier tied his hands. A chill of terror ran down Catherine's spine, "No, stop!" Catherine shrieked. Susanne and Jean Jr. ran to their mother.

Another one of the soldiers grabbed Catherine from behind and pushed her and the children toward the house. He opened the door and shoved them inside.

"What do you think you are doing? I have done nothing wrong here. This is my home, my family, my property, and you are trespassing," yelled Jean, who was struggling to ward off the men who were trying to restrain him. There was a rifle pointed at Jean's head. The soldiers were able to wrestle Jean onto a waiting horse. Then without a word, they all turned swiftly and galloped away. "Get help, Catherine!" yelled Jean.

Catherine and the children huddled by the window, and in disbelief watched the cloud of dust that arose from the horses until the last of the British soldiers and Jean were long out of sight. Terrified, Catherine tightly wrapped the children in her arms. "Where is Papa going? When will he be back? What are we going to do?" cried Jean Jr. and Susanne.

Catherine told them, "Stay in the house and let no one in while I go for help." Catherine breathlessly ran until she reached Small Eagle, a tribe member who lived close by. Between sobs, Catherine told Small Eagle that British solders took Jean away.

"I will send a runner to Chief Wabasi at St. Joseph," Small Eagle said. "Do not worry, we will find out where Jean is. We will take care of you and the children until he returns. I will send Half Day, your brother, to be with you."

But, Catherine worried; what was going to happen to Jean, to her, to the children, to their home, and the trading post? So many questions. She had no choice but to wait for answers.

CHAPTER 14

PRISONER OF WAR

The soldiers did not respond to any of Jean's questions. When they got to the lake, they transferred from the horses to waiting boats and headed up north on Lake Michigan. It was a faster route to their destination. Jean's hands were still tied, and he was aware that a gun was always focused on him.

Jean had not been to Fort Michilimackinac even though it was a large important trading depot for trappers, Indians, and people engaged in the fur trade.

The men docked their boats close to a sign that read "Water Gate."

FORT MACHILIMACKINAC
(mich ill ah mack in ah)

In 1715, French soldiers built Fort Michilimackinac as a French fur-trading village and military post on the mainland in the upper Great Lakes of North America. The village connected two massive bodies of water, Lake Huron and Lake Michigan called the Straits of Mackinac. The French gave up the fort, along with their territory in Canada to the British in 1763 following their loss in the French and Indian War. The British moved Fort Michilimackinac to a nearby island during the Revolutionary War and renamed it Fort Mackinac.

Nearby, canoes of various large sizes, 25 to 45 feet, were anchored on shore. Jean and the soldiers disembarked and passed the armed guards at the opening into the fort. Once inside, Jean was surprised to count about 15 buildings on the property. He also observed fur trading activities taking place inside one of the gates.

Jean was taken to a barracks and locked inside. He was left alone with his thoughts and worries until a guard came and led him out into the courtyard where a group of people were seated at long tables eating a meal. Jean was told to sit and eat. In his conversation with others around the table, he found that some people living at the fort were French civilians who worked there; others were British fur traders; while others were prisoners, like him. After his meal, he was led back and locked in the barracks. Exhausted from his worries and the trip, Jean slept through the night.

The next morning, Colonel Arent Schuyler de Peyster, the British commander who had ordered Jean's capture, was waiting at his office for Jean's arrival.

"Colonel de Peyster, may I present Jean Baptiste Pointe du Sable," announced Lieutenant Bennett.

The colonel dismissed Lieutenant Bennett and motioned Jean to sit in the chair across from his desk.

"So, you are the du Sable I've been hearing about. I understand that you have a home, a wife, two children, and have developed property near the Checagou portage. Is that correct, du Sable?"

"It is correct," said Jean, who spoke with quiet confidence.

"It has become apparent to us that you have been giving aid to George Rodgers Clark with the American government and his band of men, who are interfering with our ability to control the areas of the Great Lakes and the forts along the Mississippi River," continued de Peyster. "You live in a territory that is of strategic importance to us, and we fully intend to keep control of this area until and after the messy business of this war is over."

Settling back in his chair and studying Jean, the Colonel said, "I'm curious, du Sable, what did you do before you started farming and trading at your present location?"

"I worked at a trading post in St. Louis," Jean answered.

"How long were you there?" asked the Colonel.

"About three years," said Jean.

"Did you trade with trappers and Indians?" asked the Colonel.

"I did."

"Do you speak some Indian dialects?" asked the Colonel.

"I do," Jean said.

"We have some trouble-making Indians who live outside the walls of the fort and trade with our people," said the Colonel.

"I noticed," Jean replied. "I observed that the men trading with the Indians are treating them in an inferior way. Indians don't like that, and you will be the loser."

"What do you mean?" inquired the Colonel.

"The pelts I saw are not the quality that I know the Indians have," Jean replied

"Do you think that you could deal with them and improve our relations?" asked the Colonel.

"I am a prisoner here," Jean replied.

"Correct, you are a prisoner and you will be working here – for us. And we anticipate the work you do will be to our satisfaction," stated the Colonel with a tinge of threat in his voice. That is enough for today, du Sable. I am calling Lieutenant Bennett to take you back to your accommodations."

"I want to know what is happening to my wife and children," Jean said.

"Your wife and children will not be harmed. Our goal is to take the portage and not hurt anyone in the process," stated Colonel de Peyster. Jean sincerely wanted to believe that the colonel spoke the truth.

Over the next several days, Jean became more familiar with Fort Michilimackinac. It was on the tip of the mainland between two large lakes, Lake Huron and Lake Michigan. It was a fortified village with a continuous wall of wooden spikes surrounding the large campus. There were horse stables, sheep pens, and row houses inside the stockade walls. There were two guarded entrances; one on the mainland called Land Gate, and the other off the shore of Lake Michigan called the Water Gate. Soldiers patrolled both gates.

When Chief Wabasi was informed of Jean's capture, he sent Red Cloud and another scout to Ft. Michilimackinac to find and check on the conditions of their friend. Chief Wabasi gave Red Cloud fur pelts to exchange so they could get inside the compound to find Jean. When the two Indians arrived at the Water Gate entrance, they were sent to the merchant who was responsible for the exchange of goods. At his first sight of Red Cloud, Jean's heart leaped in his chest. A thin smile crossed Jean's face as he worked his way over to where the bartering of the business exchange was taking place. Not a word was spoken but through the sign language that Jean knew, Red Cloud was able to transmit that Jean's family was well in St. Joseph, and Checagou was overseen by Small Eagle.What a relief that short encounter was for Jean! He now knew his family was well and the trading post was still there.

Several weeks after Jean's arrival at the fort, he was asked to do some trading business with a group of Ottawa and Chippewa Indians who lived nearby and traded at the fort. Jean proved himself to be the right person for the job. It was a surprise to the Indian traders that a non-Indian spoke their language with such fluency and treated them with respect. After that exchange, the Indians said they would only do business with du Sable. Jean became the interpreter the British needed thanks to his facility for learning language.

Before Colonel DePeyster moved from his command at Fort Michilimackinac, he wrote in his report about Jean, "Jean Baptiste Pointe du Sable has in every way behaved in a manner becoming to a man of his station. He is a handsome Negro, well-educated, and of good character." [2]

When British Lieutenant Governor Patrick Sinclair became the new commander of Fort Michilimackinac, he was briefed about Jean. Colonel DePeyster told him that du Sable was the person to deal with the Indians in the bartering of furs at the trading post.

Jean's knowledge of Indian affairs so impressed British Governor Patrick Sinclair that he told his superiors that "du Sable is a man of intelligence and ability."[3] He is a man of experience among the Indians and more capable than anyone known to be in charge of the trading post.

Jean became the man dealing with people making trades for merchandise. Because he met canoes that arrived at the Water Gate, he was able to greet Red Cloud when he came to report on happenings at home.

"The house is closed in Chicago, but the Indians in the area are making sure nothing bad happens to your property. Catherine misses you and wants you home. She is worried that the children will not remember you," Red Cloud told Jean.

"I think of them every day and I cannot wait to return, but I fear I would be killed if I tried to escape. Governor Sinclair put me in charge of the trading post here that includes handling goods arriving in boats that come from as far as Europe. I am learning a great deal that I want to use when I get home," Jean said.

[2,3] Milo Milton Quaife, *Chicago And The Old Northwest*, 1913.

"I hear rumblings from the merchants and from around the fort that the war is not going well for the British," Jean told Red Cloud. "Maybe someday I will be out of here."

Then, it happened!! A ship docked and a man from the crew ran from the boat and handed Jean a newspaper, with the headlines:

THE WAR IS OVER!
The British surrender to the Americans.
The American Revolutionary War ends after 8 years.

The year was 1783.

Jean was on his way home. It had been three years and four months since he had seen his wife and children, and he couldn't wait to be with them!

CHAPTER 15

REUNION

The Potawatomi Indians were aware the war had ended and that Jean would be a free man. Red Cloud was sent to pick him up.

When Jean was able to leave the fort, he was told that he could take from the trading post whatever he could use at home. He took as many blankets, tools, kettles, and books as they could put in the boat.

"Why are you carrying so many books?" asked Red Cloud.

"These books are written in the English language which I learned to speak at the fort. Since the colonists won the war, English will be the language of the land. Catherine, Jean Jr., and Susanne must learn to speak English to work with the travelers who will pass through our portage and stay with us," Jean answered.

Once they were on their way home, Jean's excitement grew. He was impatient to see Catherine and the children. It seemed to be taking forever, every minute seemed a lifetime.

"Tell me, Red Cloud, so much time has passed. What has been happening?" inquired Jean.

"A new man, a white man, by the name of John Kinzie now lives among us. He is a trapper and trader who came from Detroit. He seems to get along well with our people."

On their journey Red Cloud continued to fill Jean in on events that had taken place while Jean was gone.

As they docked the canoe, Jean heard the rhythmic beat of the drums which matched the beat of his heart. Someone alerted the tribe that the welcoming festivities could begin.

A great cheer resounded throughout the camp when Red Cloud and Jean appeared. Tears of happiness streamed down Catherine's face as she ran to hug Jean, who dropped the gifts he was carrying to hug her back.

Susanne and Jean Jr. stood a short distance away unsure what to do. It had been over three years since they had seen their father, a lifetime to children so young. Catherine took Jean by the hand and walked over to the children. How they had grown and changed, thought Jean.

When Jean had last seen Jean Jr., he was nine years old. Jean Jr., now 12, was on his way to becoming a well built, handsome, young man. His hair was black and wavy, pulled back behind his head, and tied with a strip of deer hide. He was dressed like his Indian brothers. He was old enough that the younger men of the tribe had taught him to fish, snare rabbits, use a bow and arrow, and hunt deer. He was growing into manhood. Jean Jr. nodded a formal greeting to his father.

Susanne, now a 10-year-old, was still considered a little girl. She was beautiful like her mother with the same nose, brow, and soft brown eyes. Her braided hair was like black silk, her smile, wide. She wore a deerskin dress. After a few uncomfortable moments, she broke into a run that landed her in Jean's arms. He was at last in the warm embrace of his family. Jean had been waiting a very long time for this day.

The chief in his white buffalo skins appeared from his lodge, "Welcome home, Jean Baptiste, we missed you."

As Jean looked over those who had gathered, he saw all his

friends who were like family to him. Some dressed in their finest clothes decorated with porcupine quills and feathers while others had their bodies painted from head to toe. It was so good to be back! A great feast was prepared and the musicians assembled. Games, feasting, and dancing began.

CHAPTER 16

CHECAGOU

Once the festivities ended, Jean was eager to see his house. Jean helped Catherine pack the things they had accumulated. The family set out by boat to Checagou. This trip was very different from that first trip Catherine and Jean had made together. This was all conversation and excitement. For so long, Jean had wondered what Checagou would look like. Will the house be lost in weeds and brush? Would it even be there? Could they find the trading post? As they rounded the final bend in the river to catch sight of the property, Jean let out a cry, "What a beautiful sight! It is even grander than I remember!" It was there, all of it. His Indian friends had taken very good care of it.

"Catherine," Jean said with great enthusiasm, "we are going to be very successful. All my years of working, learning, traveling, and especially the time spent at Fort Michilimackinac have led to opportunities for us. We will create a welcome place for travelers who need rest and supplies for their continued journey. You and I can do this, and Jean Jr. and Susanne are old enough to be of great help.

Due to increasing trade in the Great Lakes region, their business flourished over the years. The du Sable trading post was a welcome spot for the travelers. Jean had shelves arranged with blankets, kettles, colorful bolts of cloth, guns, tomahawks, knives, and gift items of rings, bells, silver jewelry, and multi-colored beads. Indians brought in their packs of furs, hides, and tobacco to trade for these items. Catherine provided a welcoming home away from home for travelers by offering good meals and comfortable sleeping accommodations. When Jean was in Checagou and not traveling, guests could count on being entertained by storytelling, fiddle playing, and tours of the area.

After years of hard work, Jean surprised the family one night at the dinner table by saying, "It is time for us to take a break. I have been thinking about it for awhile and I'd like to take you to St. Louis to show you where I lived and first worked and have you meet friends that I still have in the area. What would you think of that? We could leave in a few weeks after the spring rains have slowed down."

Catherine, Suzanne, and Jean Jr. looked at each other. Up to this time their only travel had been to St. Joseph. This news was met with great enthusiasm. Within weeks, the four of them were in the canoe heading south to St. Louis rowing or sailing by day and camping by night making it a leisurely trip.

Through business, Jean had made new friends along the way. One was a priest, Father St. Pierre, at the Catholic Church of the Holy Family in Cahokia, Illinois, just outside of St. Louis. Jean asked Catherine if she would like to renew their wedding vows in this church and have the children be their attendants. The year was 1788. Jean and Catherine worked out arrangements with the parish priest and they were remarried in a church wedding. Jean Jr., 17, and Susanne, 15, were proud to be a part of this momentous occasion.

In continuing their trip, they moved on to St. Louis. Their first stop was the trading post. Henri was there behind the counter.

It was a pleasure to introduce Henri to his family. "You are a lucky man, Jean. You did the right thing by moving on from here. I know you have developed a trading post of your own near the Checagou portage. Someday I would like to come and see it," said Henri.

"You must come, Henri. After all, I owe you a great deal for hiring this young man and teaching him so much of the business. Believe me, you will get the royal treatment when you come. We will be expecting you," said Jean.

After they bid their goodbyes, they found that Mary and Elmer were still living in their house. Jonathan, now 25, was married and a home builder in the area. Jean was sad to learn that Etta, Mary's mother, had died a few years before. One request that Jean made was to have Mary and Elmer take them to Maggie's grave. There, Jean said a prayer for his beautiful, little friend.

Jean, Catherine, Suzanne, and Jean Jr. continued their discoveries of St. Louis with Jean telling stories of times past. They found a place to spend the night before their early departure home.

"When can we do this again?" asked the children.

CHAPTER 17

UNREST

While things continued to go well for Jean and Catherine in Checagou, their Indian neighbors and friends were being pushed from their lands and hunting grounds by American settlers. War parties were organized by the Indians to defend themselves from the intruders. Violence erupted with regularity. Peace negotiations with the government were failing.

American leadership was in the hands of the first President of the United States, George Washington. He chose a man, a military hero during the American Revolutionary War, to gather soldiers to stop the Indians' uprisings.

THE BATTLE OF FALLEN TIMBERS – 1794

After the American Revolution of 1775-1783, the United States maintained that the Indian nations no longer owned the lands they had lived on for centuries. The Indians resisted the encroaching American settlers moving onto their territory, flattening forests, and depleting their source of food. President George Washington engaged an American Revolutionary hero, General "Mad" Anthony Wayne, to gather an army to fight the warring Indians.

A major battle was fought between Indian warriors from numerous tribes against a much larger, better trained American army at a place called Fallen Timbers. The Indians were defeated.

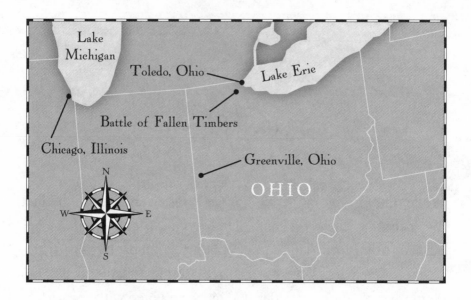

General "Mad" Anthony Wayne put together an army and made arrangements to meet the warring Indians at a location called Fallen Timbers, a place where a tornado had blown down hundreds of large hardwood trees. (near today's Toledo, Ohio) The Indians were confident of victory; however, when they joined in fierce combat, over days of conflict, Indian warriors (1,500) from numerous tribes were defeated by a much larger (2,500), better trained American army.

THE GREENVILLE TREATY

Over 1,000 Indian warriors and chiefs gathered on August 3, 1795
to sign the Treaty of Greenville (present-day Greenville, Ohio)
as a result of losing the Battle of Fallen Timbers. In the treaty,
the Indians agreed to give up much of their land.
Among the locations the Indians surrendered to the
United States were large parts of modern-day Ohio,
Fort Detroit, and the future site of downtown Chicago.

As a result of the Indians' defeat, The Greenville Treaty was written by the American government. Over 1,000 Indian warriors from ten different Indian tribes gathered on August 3, 1795 to sign the treaty in Greenville, Ohio. Included in the treaty, the Potawatomi gave to the United States a tract of land six miles square at the mouth of the Checagou River, present day downtown Chicago.

Over the next few years, skirmishes continued to break out. After so many generations of independence, the Potawatomi realized that life as they knew it would never be the same. The white man was flattening forests and removing food supplies.

When Potawatomi friends left St. Joseph to resettle, Catherine and Jean felt the pain of it. By the time Catherine's parents were contemplating their move to Peoria, Illinois, Catherine began talking about the possibility for Jean and her to follow.

About that same time, Jean heard talk of a fort being built at the mouth of the Checagou River by the United States government to protect the Americans. Fort Dearborn was to be erected right across the river from his home. Jean did not like the idea of the fort. Over the years, he had developed a substantial amount of property. He and the people who worked for him were doing just fine without the United States Army moving in next door.

Late one night, Catherine and Jean sat down for a long talk.

"Catherine, we have built our life here. But we are older and this place has outgrown us. Let us sell what we have and use the money to start over in Peoria. Jean Jr. and I can farm doing just enough to sustain ourselves; no more hard work for you, no more traveling for me. We will be with family and friends. Susanne and husband Jean Pelletier, and our granddaughter, Eulalie live in St. Charles, Missouri near St. Louis. We want to be closer to them. This IS what we have been talking about, isn't it, Catherine?"

"Yes," Catherine said with a deep sigh. She was tired of thinking and talking. "I am ready," she said.

After all the discussions with Catherine and Jean Jr., Jean Baptiste Pointe du Sable was ready to make the move to Peoria, Illinois.

Jean La Lime was a younger man who worked for Jean at the trading post and the portage. Jean knew that he wanted to stay in the area, but he knew that La Lime did not have the money to buy the property, though La Lime seemed to have the backing of someone who did. John Kinzie, the trapper and trader who lived among the Potawatomi in St. Joseph was witness to the bill of sale and three years later bought the du Sable estate.

In 1800, Jean sold his home and property to Jean La Lime.

An inventory of some of the personal holdings of du Sable at the time of the sale included:

> The log home 22 feet by 40 feet
>
> Interior furnishings: a French walnut cabinet with four glass doors 8 feet by 4 feet
>
> A feather bed, paintings, chairs, mirrors, copper kettles
>
> 2 barns, a workshop, a horse stable, a hen house, a bake house, a dairy
>
> 32 cows, 28 hogs, 44 hens, 2 mules
>
> Plows, carts, axes, saws, sickles, scythes[4]

Three years later John Kinzie bought the du Sable estate. The Kinzie people stayed and prospered in Chicago. Until more recent information about du Sable surfaced, Kinzie had been credited with being called the "Father of Chicago." But Jean Baptisite Pointe du Sable settled there many years before John Kinzie. It is Jean Baptiste Pointe du Sable who is now rightfully recognized as the "Father of Chicago."

Some reminders of Jean Baptiste Pointe du Sable:

> A Du Sable High School
>
> A Du Sable granite headstone on his grave in St. Charles Borromeo Cemetery
>
> A Du Sable Museum
>
> A Du Sable National Historic Landmark in Pioneer Plaza
>
> A Du Sable United States commemorative postal stamp
>
> A Du Sable bronze statue on the NE side of the Michigan Avenue Bridge
>
> A Du Sable Bridge – formerly known as the Michigan Avenue Bridge

---

[4] Historian Milo M. Quaife, discovered the bill of sale from du Sable to Jean La Lime archived in Detroit, Michigan.

EPILOGUE

This brings an end to our story of Jean Baptiste Pointe du Sable, a young man from Santo Domingo with an adventurous spirit who is credited with being the "Father of Chicago." Unlike others who had come before him, he set down roots and established a permanent location that grew to become the city of Chicago, one of the major cities of the world.

After Catherine died in Peoria, Jean and Jean Jr. moved to St. Charles, Missouri to be close to Jean's granddaughter, Eulalie.

Fortune was not kind to du Sable toward the end of his life and he died a poor man in 1818. But before he died, he made sure that Eulalie would have him buried in the St. Charles Borromeo Cemetery in St. Charles, Missouri where a granite headstone marks his grave today.

For decades, du Sable's work and dedication to this area we call Chicago were lost. It was years before anyone recognized that Jean Baptiste Pointe du Sable was the first to settle this area. He had the vision of Chicago being a crossroads that would grow. He is now rightfully recognized as the "Father of Chicago."

We are grateful for his life, his dedication and his contribution to our lives, and our American story.

TIMELINE I

JEAN BAPTISTE POINT DU SABLE

<table>
<tr><td>

</td><td>

1745
Jean Baptiste Pointe du Sable is born in Santo Domingo.

</td></tr>
</table>

1762
Jean leaves Santo Domingo and sets sail for
New Orleans, Louisiana.

1764
Jean works in the fur trading business in St. Louis, Missouri.

1767
Jean moves to a Potawatomi Indian village in
St. Joseph, Michigan.

1769
Jean marries Catherine, a Potawatomi Indian from the
St. Joseph Village, and moves to Checagou (Chicago)
to establish a trading post.

1771
Jean Baptiste Pointe du Sable Jr. is born.

1773
Susanne du Sable is born.

1779
Jean is arrested by the British during the American Revolutionary
War and taken to Fort Michilimackinac.

1783
At the end of the war, Jean returns to his trading post
in Checagou.

1788
Jean and Catherine travel 280 miles to Cahokia, Missouri
to marry in a catholic church.

1790
Susanne du Sable marries Jean Pelletier.

1796
Eulalie Pelletier, daughter of Susanne and Jean Pelletier, is born.

1800
Jean sells his Checagou property to Jean la Lime.

Jean and Catherine move to Peoria, Illinois.

1804
John Kinzie, sometimes called the "Father of Chicago," buys the du Sable property from Jean la Lime.

1805
Catherine dies and is buried in Peoria, Illinois.

1807
Jean and his son, Jean Jr. move to St. Charles, Missouri to be close to Jean's granddaughter, Eulalie.

1818
Jean dies and is buried in the St. Charles Borremeo Cemetery in St. Charles, Missouri.

1934
The Du Sable High School opens in Bronzeville, a neighborhood of Chicago.

1965
A plaza called Pioneer Court is built on the north side of the Michigan Avenue Bridge near the location of du Sable's former home and trading post.

1968
During Illinois' 150th birthday, Chicago city leaders place a headstone at du Sable's unmarked grave in the St. Borremeo Cemetery in St. Charles, Missouri.

1973
The Du Sable Museum of African-American History opens at 740 E. 56th Place.

1976
The previous homesite of du Sable is designated a National Historic Landmark in Pioneer Court.

1987

A Jean Baptiste Pointe du Sable commemorative 22-cent stamp is issued by the U.S. Postal Service as part of the Black Heritage Series.

Jean Baptiste Pointe du Sable ©1987 USPS. All Rights Reserves. Used with permission.

2000

2009

Erik Blome, a Chicago artist, sculpts a bronze bust of Du Sable.

2010

The Michigan Avenue Bridge at the Chicago River is renamed the Du Sable Bridge. The Du Sable bust stands on the NE corner of the Du Sable Bridge at Pioneer Court.

TIMELINE II

1700s – 1900s

1700

1776
The 13 American colonies declare war against the British Government, starting the American Revolutionary War.

1776
The Declaration of Independence is drafted by Thomas Jefferson.

1783
The American colonists win full independence from the British Government.

1789
George Washington becomes the first president of the United States.

1795
The Potawatomi Indians sign the Greenville Treaty, giving up six square miles of land at the mouth of the Chicago River to the American Government.

1800

1803
Emperor Napoleon Bonaparte of France sells New Orleans, Louisiana and most of the land west of the Mississippi River to the United States for $15 million.

1803
Thomas Jefferson, the third president of the United States, orders a fort built in Chicago to protect the settlers from the Indians. Fort Dearborn is to be built on the south side of the Chicago River, across from the du Sable property.

1812
Fort Dearborn is burned to the ground by Potawatomi Indians and their allies.

1818
Illinois becomes the twenty-first state of the United States.

1833
Chicago is incorporated as a town, becoming the largest in the Midwest.

1861
The Civil War begins between the northern and southern states in America.

1871
Most of the city of Chicago is destroyed by fire in areas we today call the Loop, Old Town, the Gold Coast, and more. Hundreds of people died and 200,000 were left homeless.

1893
Chicago hosts a World's Fair, The Columbian Exposition, celebrating the 400th anniversary of Christopher Columbus' discovery of America. The greatest among the many attractions was the Ferris Wheel. It held 2,160 passengers at once. Each car held 60 people. Twenty-seven million visitors attend over its six months opening.

1933
Chicago celebrates its 100th birthday with a fair called the Century of Progress. A replica of du Sable's cabin is included at the fair.

1900

ACKNOWLEDGEMENTS

I never intended to write a book; it just happened gradually.

After moving to downtown Chicago, I was asked by an acquaintance if I would join a group that was forming to volunteer at an inner-city elementary grade school in the Cabrini Green Housing Projects. I did.

I was paired with an excellent young teacher who was getting her Master's degree in education. I looked forward to working with her and the children.

One day, the principal of the school mentioned to me that she wished someone would write a book about Jean Baptiste Pointe du Sable, the black man who is credited with being called the "Father of Chicago." The title had previously been given to John Kinzie, a white trapper and trader who came to Chicago in 1803.

This started me on my journey of research which included a trip to St. Charles Borromeo Cemetery in St. Charles, Missouri and meeting with Potawatomi leaders in St. Joseph, Michigan. With starts and stops over twenty years, I worked on this project. It seemed people would be well served by being aware of this history.

Years later, I found that school principal and gave her my manuscript to read. She encouraged me to move forward. Others who have critiqued, and offered suggestions are many: my editor, Liz Schwab: Betty Woodward, Audrey West, Potawatomi educators, my writing group, Jan Franck, Jody Vorbrich, Joan and Wes Boldt, Janice Todd, D Clancy, Liz Garvey, Joanne Ellis, Mary Jo Graham, Rosemary Olds, Michael Harrington, Sue Jensen, Charlie and Yvonne Carroll, Robert Bannister, Patrick Monaghan, Kari Greenfield, Hugh Kennedy, Lynette Carver, Greg Morrill, Erik Blome, sculptor of du Sable, and most importantly, my husband Bob Beh.

SOURCE NOTES

Little is known about Chicago's early days because the fire of 1871 destroyed much of Chicago's past: city documents, manuscripts, records, and books.

My research has taken me many places, but I take what I have learned about du Sable's life primarily from the research done by Milo Milton Quaife who wrote CHICAGO AND THE OLD NORTHWEST, originally published in 1913.

Mr. Quaife was born in 1880 and received a Ph.D from the University of Chicago. He became a professor at Chicago's Lewis Institute of Technology, editor of the State Historical Society of Wisconsin, editor of the Burton Historical Collection at the Detroit Public Library. All this time he was researching the early days of Chicago and the Midwest. He included a sophisticated interpretation of Du Sable's importance.